Raphael

SCALA

RAPHAEL
(Urbino 1483 - Rome 1520)

Raphael was born into an artistic family in Urbino, where at an early age he entered the workshop of his father, the painter Giovanni Santi. In 1500 he was already described as an independent "master" in a document, and as such moved frequently between his native city and other centers (Città di Castello, Perugia, Venice). Four years later, with a letter of introduction from the duchess of Urbino, he went to Florence "to learn." And it was here in fact that he came into contact with the art of Leonardo, assimilating its balance and sobriety of composition. In this period he painted pictures of religious subjects and portraits for great Florentine families (portraits of *Agnolo Doni* and *Maddalena Strozzi Doni*): the figures that he immortalized were from the outset characterized by profound psychological insight, revealing not just the social status of the sitters, but also the fundamental traits of their personality. His pictures of the Madonna also display a deeply human intensity of emotions and a serenity in her relationship with her son which

Madonna di Foligno, detail
Pinacoteca, Vatican

Self-Portrait
Uffizi, Florence

observers are always made to feel they share in. Discovered by Bramante, then architect to the papal court, he was summoned to Rome by Julius II in 1508 to fresco the Stanze in the Vatican: the artist left the *Madonna del Baldacchino* incomplete in Florence in order to carry out the work commissioned by such a prestigious client. In Rome Raphael surrounded himself with collaborators in order to meet his numerous commitments, to the popes Julius II and then Leo X, as well as to other illustrious figures of the time (portrait of *Baldassarre Castiglione*, fresco of the *Galatea* for Agostino Chigi's Villa Farnesina). At the papal court he worked not only as a painter but also as a city planner and "architect of the fabric of St. Peter's." He drew up a plan in relief of ancient Rome and designed some important buildings, like Villa Madama.

The frescoes for the Stanze bear witness to his extraordinary ability to rework the

The Prophet Isaiah, detail Sant'Agostino, Rome

models of classicism as well as those of his contemporaries (Leonardo, Michelangelo, Bramante), to whom he paid tribute by including their portraits in the majestic setting of the *School of Athens*. The scenes representing biblical and historical episodes or allegories and concepts of philosophy and theology eloquently illustrate the painter's skill in rendering ideas of universal significance concrete and relevant to his own time. Little is known of his private life: the working-class woman "much loved by him until his death," in Vasari's words, is depicted in numerous works, including the *Donna Velata* and the celebrated *Fornarina* (so-called after the trade pursued by her father, the *fornaio* or baker Francesco Luti), who wears a bracelet inscribed with the painter's name.

Raphael met a premature death in 1520, at the age of only thirty-seven. His epitaph, written by the Humanist Pietro Bembo, speaks of a competition on equal terms between the painter and nature: "This is that Raphael, by whom in life / Our mighty mother Nature fear'd defeat; / And in whose death did fear herself to die."

Fire in the Borgo, detail Stanza dell'Incendio di Borgo, Vatican

5

**ADORATION
OF THE MAGI,**
detail of the
Oddi Altarpiece
Pinacoteca, Vatican

**ST GEORGE
AND THE DRAGON**
Louvre, Paris

**THE MARRIAGE
OF THE VIRGIN**,
details
Pinacoteca di Brera,
Milan
(pages 8-11)

**PORTRAIT OF
A YOUNG WOMAN**
(*Lady with
a Unicorn*), details
Galleria Borghese,
Rome

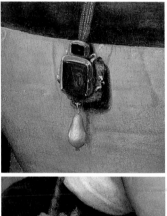

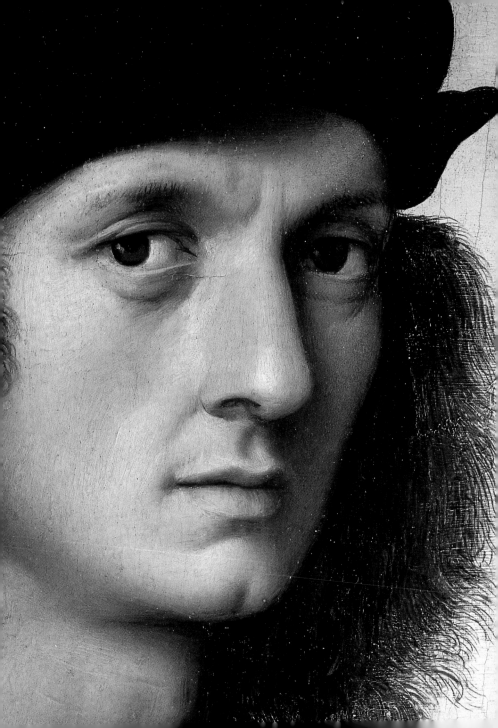

**PORTRAITS
OF AGNOLO AND
MADDALENA DONI,**
details
Galleria Palatina,
Florence
(pages 14-17)

**STUDY FOR
THE DEPOSITION
OF CHRIST**, detail
Gabinetto dei Disegni
e delle Stampe,
Uffizi, Florence

**DEPOSITION
OF CHRIST**, details
Galleria Borghese,
Rome
(pages 19-23)

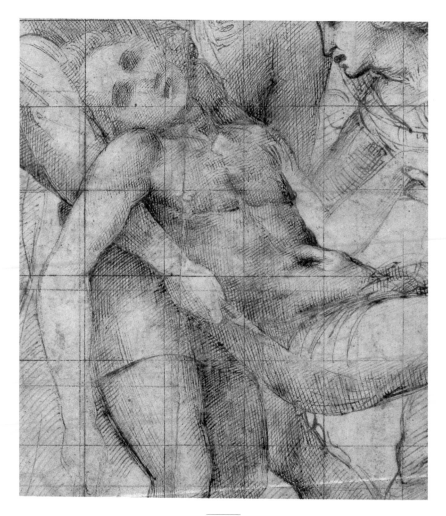

**THE CANIGIANI
HOLY FAMILY**,
details
Alte Pinakothek,
Munich

MADONNA DEL BALDACCHINO,
details
Galleria Palatina,
Florence

SCHOOL OF ATHENS,
details
Stanza della
Segnatura, Vatican
(pages 28-35)

FIRE IN THE BORGO,
details
Stanza dell'Incendio
di Borgo, Vatican
(pages 36-39)

PORTRAIT
OF A CARDINAL,
detail
Prado, Madrid

PORTRAIT OF
FEDRA INGHIRAMI,
detail
Galleria Palatina,
Florence

LOGGIA OF PSYCHE
Villa Farnesina,
Rome

**TRIUMPH
OF GALATEA**, details
Villa Farnesina,
Rome
(pages 43-47)

**PORTRAIT
OF A WOMAN**
(*La Donna Velata*),
details
Galleria Palatina,
Florence

**MADONNA AND CHILD
WITH THE INFANT
SAINT JOHN** (*Madonna
della Seggiola*), detail
Galleria Palatina,
Florence
(pages 50-51)

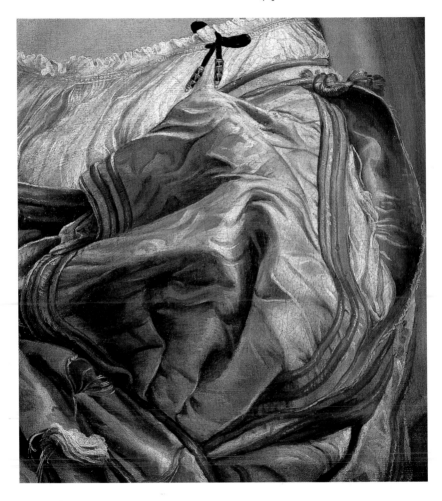

DOUBLE PORTRAIT, detail
Louvre, Paris

PORTRAIT OF BALDASSARRE CASTIGLIONE, detail
Louvre, Paris

PORTRAIT OF LEO X WITH TWO CARDINALS, detail
Uffizi, Florence
(pages 54-55)

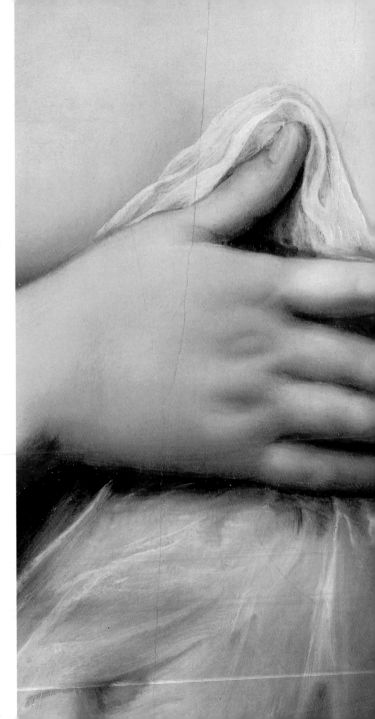

PORTRAIT OF A WOMAN
(*La Fornarina*),
detail
Galleria Nazionale
d'Arte Antica, Rome

School of Raphael,
details of the fresco
decoration of the
SECOND LOGGIA
Vatican

Cupid Drawn by Serpents

"Stufetta" of Cardinal Bibbiena, Vatican

The illustrations in this volume have been supplied
by the SCALA PICTURE LIBRARY,
the largest source of color transparencies and digital images
of the visual arts in the world.
The over 60,000 subjects visible at the site
www.scalarchives.it
can be accessed through computerized procedures
that permit easy and rapid picture searches of any complexity.

e-mail: archivio@scalagroup.com

Text by: Maria Caterina Pincherle
Translation: Huw Evans
Layout: Studio Contri Toscano
Photographs: SCALA Picture Library

The images from the SCALA Picture Library
reproducing cultural assets that belong to the Italian State
are published with the permission of the
Ministry for Cultural Heritage and Activities

Printed by: D'Auria Industrie Grafiche S.p.A.,
Ascoli Piceno, 2004